"IRISH JEW…

AND OTHER TALES OF

LIFE IN THE JUDY LANE"

By Judy Lane

In Memory Of
Peter Ricky Lane
1958-1984
My baby brother, Petie

Table of Contents

JUDY LANE

Things You Need to Know

If anyone would have told me when I was a frightened 7-year old throwing up the Holy Host at my first Communion that I would grow up to find out I was actually Jewish, marry a man and after more than a dozen years of marriage, fall in love with my soul mate—-another woman, go on to have a baby by artificial insemination at 44 and adopt another child at 46, appear on a reality show on national TV, get married again at nearly 55 to that woman, all the while leading a typical all-American family life, I would have told them they were crazy. And, so maybe they were crazy--but nonetheless right, because I am and here's my story:

Irish Jew and other tales of Life in the Judy Lane

These few stories come out of literally hundreds that I have written and published since 1996 when I was brought on by Universal Press Syndicate allegedly to fill the hole left by the inimitable Erma Bombeck. That lasted only two short years as the newspaper editors grieving process for a one-of-a-kind wit outlasted the patience at UPS. I went on to self-syndicate a weekly column, which has after 10 years turned into a monthly venture called, "Life in the Judy Lane."

I've attempted to put these selected stories in some sort of logical order. And, why? My life certainly was nothing like that. But, I tried. The family section has been separated into two books—-much like the Old Testament and the New. Hey, I'm the product of catholic priests and nuns on one side of the family and Rabbis on the other. It seems fitting.

"In the Beginning" is life with my Irish mother and Hungarian father, who met in England during the World War II.

JUDY LANE

They immigrated to the United States in 1949 with five children under the age of 9 and one on the way. Fortunately for me, my parents were madly in love with one another and went on to have two more, myself and my younger brother, Petie—affectionately known to the rest of the family as "the Americans."

I was born in the lower eastside of Manhattan and grew up in a public housing project in the Bronx. Later my father at 58, when other Dads are considering retirement gathered up the family to move to "God's country," aka California and begin again.

"Come to Mama" includes stories of my own parenting, as I share life with my partner and now wife (thanks to the good people of the State of California) of 21 years, Pepper, our son, Cory 11-1/2 and daughter Shea 9.

To us, our family is no different than the Cleavers, the Andersons, the Nelsons or any other sitcom TV family we both grew up with—-only this time June hooks up with Harriet to raise a child born through artificial insemination and another adopted by pure divine intervention.

The final chapter is simply "Life in the Judy Lane," which includes a random collection of columns that seemed to hit a chord with my regulars on my "friends and family" list for my column.

I hope you laugh, cry, drop your jaw, shut your mouth, any kind of emotion. Just for a few minutes for each story, get away from your own life and travel with me in the Judy Lane.

Acknowledgments

The remarkable Hillary Clinton said it best, "It takes a village..." The following is my village for this book.

Michele Humphrey is an amazing, creative genius and more importantly, my friend. She took a wild vision in my head and recreated it for the cover of my book. She does more than just capture what you want, she delves into your psyche and spirit to pull out what you need and don't even know you do. The cover is just another of Michele's magic she has shared with me and now with all of you.

Every woman needs a mentor. Fortunately for me, I found mine when I was 21 years old and naively thought I couldn't possibly know more than I did at that moment. I was getting married to my boyfriend of three years and all set to buy my first home. What could anyone teach me that I didn't already know?

Enter Charon D'Aiello Sandoval to slap some sense into me. For the next 34 years, this amazing woman alternately guided, nurtured, loved, liked, advised, consoled, and scolded me, effectively helping turn me into the makings of an amazing woman. We shall see——I still have a few years to go, hopefully.

Charon has taken the stories herein and helped organize them into some semblance of order. I am forever grateful to my dear friend and mentor for this and so much more.

For the past dozen years or more, I have had a faithful following that I have coined, "My Friends and Family List" These are the people who have allowed me into their homes weekly for ten years and for the past couple of years, each month, when I send my latest installment of "Life in the Judy

Lane." It is through these people and their "fan" letters to me that I have managed to narrow down my stories into just a few from literally hundreds that I have written.

I could not write my story without including the people who are my witnesses to events as they happened—or at least as I saw them—my brothers and sisters, Noel, Eleanor, Allan, Frankie, Mickie and Sally. They endured, enjoyed and survived along with me. Most profoundly, during the loss of our youngest brother, Petie and our beloved parents. They know better than anyone what it means for a little girl from the Bronx to end up where I am today. I'm still amazed.

To my brother-in-law Charlie Furey, who called me one day and said, "Judy, you have to write a book! It's your calling." I have known Charlie since I was nine-years old and he began dating my oldest sister, Eleanor. I love Charlie like a brother, without the need for revenge for all the crap those guys pulled. Charlie is a prince.

To the two strangers who made it possible for me to experience the joy of motherhood twice. The unknown sperm donor whose application jumped off the page at us and made us fall in love when choosing the father for our son, Cory and the brave young woman who surrendered Shea to us so that her baby girl would have two parents and a good life. We will forever treasure the gifts they gave us.

To life-long friends and my San Francisco contingent, "Zombie" Janice Acton and her husband, "The Godfather" Mark Beskind and our very own "Uncle" Daniel Abbott. They are family and have seen me at my worst and still take my calls. They have and always are there for me and the children.

To my best friend, Laurie Vargas for being that kind of friend. The one who makes you laugh till you lose drops and who shares the kinds of stories with you that can only be told when you're so old that no one would believe you. She and I endured the loss of Petie, who was her fiancé when he died 25 years ago at the age of 25.

There are sisters and there are sister-friends. These are the people who are with you because they want to be, not because you were born to the same family. Patti Adams is my sister-friend. The most amazing aunt to our children and the most incredible friend to Pepper and me. Patti saw me through one of my darkest hours...days...weeks...months and I treasure and love her for that and so much more.

To my parents who made me what I am with no excuses. As a parent myself, I realize the incredible sacrifices they made to see that I had what I needed. They provided me with an invisible net of security that has been the foundation all my growing years and long after they were gone. I knew they would always be there for me—-together and with unconditional love. I am them—the best and the worst and everything in between—and I am eternally grateful to these two courageous people.

Everything I do is for the benefit and love of our children, Cory and Shea. Everyday they make me a better person. They are my moral compass, my joy and reason for living. And, more importantly, for living right. There is no joy more intense or profound than a mother's love for her children and yet, I feel these two amazing angels have transcended me to a place of sheer joy beyond even that.

And, now as they say, I've saved the best for last. To my partner and wife and love of my life, Pepper. I have often said that I've known Pepper all my life because I just started living when I met her. Before Pepper, I only existed. She has brought color into my black and white world. She pushed me and continues to push me in all the right directions. She is the reason I am a mother, an accomplished writer and a whole and complete person. My love for her can only be compared to what my father felt for my mother—-almost to the point of obsession, but completely warranted.

This book is dedicated to you, darling Pepper. Like everything else, you're the reason it's here.

JUDY LANE

In The Beginning

JUDY LANE

"If the shoe fits..."

It was clear at our house when the first day of school was approaching. My mother would start singing and skipping around the house about a week before. After spending a long, hot summer with eight kids, I'm sure she was looking forward to her vacation.

More than I dreaded that first day back, I shuddered at the thought of shopping for new clothes. Why? Why would a kid balk at the opportunity to get new duds? You would not understand unless you had to shop with my father--the mad Hungarian.

You know you're in trouble when you go shopping at a place called "Cheap Heshey's," one of many little shops along Orchard Street in the Lower Eastside of Manhattan, where I was born. Vendors would display clothing stacked high in front of their stores, much like what you'd see at a yard sale today.

The words "style" and "comfort" were not in my father's vocabulary. Instead the theme was "sturdy" and "varm" as though we were prepared to go to battle in Siberia rather than make it back and forth to school each day.

I eyeballed the cool, trendy Peacoat that anyone who was anyone was wearing those days. Just as I reached for one, his voice rang out.

"Put dis vun on," he directed as he fitted me with a big, boxy green corduroy number that just screamed 'fat, dumpy, nerdy girl'.

The reflection in the mirror is etched in my memory. I looked like a big, green, Rubbermaid® trash barrel.

"Pretend you're holding your books now," he continued as he had me extend my arms out to clutch the imaginary load–as though I didn't already have enough room in that coat to stash my little brother.

As if this wasn't humiliating enough, he now had to bargain with Cheap Heshey to get a better deal on this gem.   After arguing, dropping the clothes down and walking away, spewing off a few Hungarian death threats and then finally returning and arguing some more, they finally agreed on a price.

"Jooody," my father would say with a smile, "you think you could take Cheap Heshey?"

Take him? I could eat peanuts off the guy's head. He was the size of a lawn jockey. Of course I could take him. But, please Daddy; I'm a little girl in a big green coat dying of embarrassment. Can we go now?

I bid farewell to my Peacoat and we were off to buy me "a shoe," as my father would describe them despite the fact that they came in twos. I don't know why he bothered to even take me along. He knew my size and he knew exactly what I was getting. Why torture me with the fantasy of all those choices? There was only one "shoe," for me. It was the "shoe" issued by parochial schools everywhere. The "shoe" not required by the public school I attended. The dreaded black and white saddle "shoe." Not because it was cool looking or remotely girlish, but because it was "sturdy." My poor father was always looking out for me. Who knows when I'd find myself on a force march and would be grateful for that "shoe."

And so on the first day of school, I'd show up looking like a human recycling bin in indestructible shoes, hoping that a crazed thief would put a gun to my head and demand, "Your clothes or your life!"

But alas, that fantasy did not come true either. And, just as my father planned, my "shoe" and the rest of my sturdy gear lasted through rain, sleet, hail and dead of night, with only the blessing of time allowing me to finally avoid this yearly ritual. I vowed when I was "big" to do two things. Buy myself a peacoat and take Cheap Hershey down. Well, one out of two isn't bad.

JUDY LANE

"Irish Jew"

"The last to know."

A perfectly appropriate cliché. Everyone seems to know that your husband's been fooling around with that twit years before you even notice that you haven't had sex since Nixon was in office.

So, here I was. The last to know at 30 when my father suddenly announces he is Jewish.

"I knew it!" my friend Charon screamed. "I've always said that there's something special about you."

Charon, who is half-Hungarian Jew and half-Italian Catholic explained everything. Because her mother was Jewish, she said, she was also. But, when it's on the paternal side, it doesn't count.

Still she knew. It never occurred to me that you could know these things about people without distinctive last names like Schwartz, Bernstein, or Katz.

My Ireland-born and raised Catholic mother had just died of cancer. Profoundly grief stricken, my Hungarian father ushered me aside and handed me a black and white photo of two strangers.

"Dese are your grendperents," he said in his thick accent.

The woman was stern with familiar features. And the man, a Rabbi. Wow. When Daddy goes Jewish he doesn't fool around. Not just kinda Jewish. Or Madonna Jewish. But, Rabbi Jewish.

My seven siblings were equally confused, stunned, tickled and in one case, angered about "Daddy's religion."

Looking back like the scorned woman, the signs were there. Mummy made Matzoballs and chicken soup that would make a rabbinical student weep. It didn't occur to us that this was anything more than a meal. But, in whispers she chided us, "don't say anything," as she gathered up boxes from the Passover display at the grocery store. So, it went into the same slot with everything else we questioned silently but never spoke of; such as what was our mother's real name? Was it Betty, which is what the neighbors called her? Or, Bridget, as my father called her? Or Agnes, which is what her sisters called her? And, was she in the witness protection program? We wondered, but obediently zipped our lips.

There was that certain sensibility around my father. The wry, witty humor, the focus on education, his liberal views and so vocal about other things gentiles seemed too uptight to discuss.

"Be cerfool who you sleep vit," he'd call out as we left for the evening. "You may hev to merry dem."

That was the sex talk. But it was more than my friends got. The message was clear. Sex was normal and expected but came with risks; something we would naturally do, but just be "wery, wery, cerfool" doing it.

And while the rest of the neighborhood tormented poor Ruthie, a wildly eccentric mother, my father's reaction would suggest sympathy instead of ridicule. Ruthie changed into a swimsuit in her car when firefighters turned on the hydrants for kids on hot, summer days and intentionally sauntered past a group of young men with her crimson lips pouted like Elke Sommer, wearing a dress two sizes too small, cotton-candy hair and mascara streaked down the side of her face, screaming,

"Stop undressing me with your eyes!"

Instead of joining in the group taunts, my father indulged

our empathy and tolerance for "de poor ting."

Clearly, it was more than just "Daddy's religion."

Although I was raised Catholic, made my sacraments, most of the venial and even a couple of mortal sins, I attended public school in New York City. Long before PC was in Merriam-Webster, we sang Jewish songs at Hanukkah along with Christmas carols, all the while envying the fact that they celebrated for eight days instead of just one. We listened rapt as classmates practiced for Bar Mitzvahs and marveled at how much dough they raked in for this accomplishment. On High Holy days, the only kids at school were Puerto Rican, Black and me. Most white Catholics went to parochial school. I didn't quite fit anywhere. To make matters worse, I had some kind of an accent.

This was particularly noticeable when our family moved to California when I was 14. But, that was a New York accent. Somehow, between my mother's Irish brogue and my father's Bela Lugosi routine, I ended up with some kind of accent that made even New Yorkers laugh.

I was 16 before I realized that that my father's favorite swear word was not spelled b-o-s-t-i-t, but rather, b-a-s-t-a-r-d. All I every heard was, "Those bleddy bostits are et it agen!" as he'd rage at some government official on TV.

Clearly, this new development regarding my father was not just about Judaism and its rituals. It was about the Jewish experience. The humor, the angst, the insufferable suffering one imposes on oneself. It's Woody Allen, Jackie Mason and David Steinberg all rolled into one. Only Jews—and some Italians— can master that. I told Charon I was getting the hang of this half Irish and half Jewish thing.

"I get drunk and feel so guilty about it the next day," I told her.

Along with the cracked photographs my father shared, came horrendous stories. Horrific and unspeakable and clearly the reason he was, well, the way he was.

Crippling fear, sadness and survivor guilt weighed him down. He became his own worst enemy. He was volatile. Out of nowhere, he would rise up and crash a thunderous rage in your direction for no apparent reason. Something you had done or not done that went unnoticed or without repercussion until it built up inside of him like a fat lady in a pair of XS Spanks™. Something had to give.

And, yet he could be tender. His heavy, calloused hand resting on your fevered head like a poor man's thermometer.

"You vill live," he'd assure you.

Meanwhile, you weren't sure if you should be relieved or terrified. Was there a chance you could have died? I thought it was just the flu? When was somebody going to tell I was at death's door?

On those rare occasions when he spoke of his own childhood, he would stop mid-sentence and weep. To be continued. . . or not. Some incidents were too hard to recount.

But, once my mother, his buffer, was gone, the flood gates opened. He shared everything.

Some of his stories were astounding. Some heartwarming. Some were just, as the kids say, too much information.

"You're talking about my mother, Daddy, please!" I'd scream as I put up a hand hoping to deflect the flurry of words regaling their apparently robust love life.

Just what I wanted to hear. First, I find out I'm Jewish—- well, almost--and now you're going to tell me my parents had sex?

Here, there and everywhere? How much can one woman take?

Once he retrieved those dormant memories, there was no reining them in. Each day brought more.

His sisters were killed in concentration camps. Shot at point-blank range, desperately clutching their children in their arms. His only brother was shot on a force march because he couldn't get back up on his feet fast enough. The only survivor besides him, was the youngest sister. She was at the opposite end of those mysterious phone calls he would get every once in a great while, where he pulled the phone into the closed bedroom and spoke Hungarian for an hour or more. She was my parents' sponsor when they came to America in 1949 with five children and one on the way.

My sister, my younger brother and I were affectionately referred to as "The Americans," by the rest of the family. Little did we know, we were Jewish-Americans. Sorta.

But, these were not just stories from books you checked out of the library. They were my uncle, aunts and cousins. The same sort of people with whom my friends celebrated the holidays. This was not a Spielberg movie I could chose not to see. There was no turning this channel. Or my father.

He began dying the moment my mother took her last breath. He was simply and completely in love with this woman.

"Der ver bettah lookahs, zome vit more mahney, but I luft her abuf all," he said, recounting his unpopular decision to choose a shiksa over perfectly suitable Jewish suitors.

The moment he saw her, he was smitten. He impulsively kissed her on the nose. He got a job where she worked. He moved into an apartment across the street from hers. Terribly romantic if you think about it. Today, I think we call this stalking.

I wanted to write to Elizabeth Kubler-Ross asking her to add a chapter, "The Deranged Bereaved" to cover what was happening to my father. When he lost my mother, he lost his way and his mind.

When our mother died, we had her entombed. My father oversaw the entire process long after the rest of our mourners had gone home to grieve. He wanted to be sure they put the right body in right crypt.

Later he told me that I when I wanted to talk to her, I should go around back to since she went in head first and there was no point in talking to her feet.

Day after day for months, he would set up his lawn chair behind the mausoleum in front of an X he etched on the back of her tomb, where he estimated her head rested. After long conversations with her, he would go into the office and make himself a nice cup of coffee. He became a regular at cemetery.

His demise was further hastened by the tragic loss of his youngest son, Petie, nine months to the day of our mother's death.

"Mummy," my father called out to the crypt. "Our beby boy is in trrrouble."

And surely he was. Just as the Nazis murdered my uncle, aunts and cousins, the equally sinister force of cancer slowly tortured and ultimately killed my baby brother. Although a handsome, strapping young man of 25, Petie was still the little knucklehead I grew up with. The one who instinctively, though unadvisedly, slapped our father on the back of his head when he slammed on the brakes of his '57 Buick and sent Petie flying up against the back of the front seat.

"Kill him, Mum!" my father shrieked, struggling to

maintain control of the wheel.

"We'll kill him latah, dahling," my mother replied calmly in her lilting Irish brogue, stroking his stinging head.

So, it was not surprising when soon after Petie passed, my father died of a broken heart. All dressed up in his grey suit and off for a night of chess at the local club, he collapsed and died instantly.

Studying him as he lay at the morgue just hours later, I was struck. I wiped my eyes to be sure I was actually seeing what I was seeing. He was more peaceful than I had ever seen him before. The deep lines of worry that etched his face were simply gone.

So much suffering for one man to endure. He lost his siblings and son under cruel and inhuman circumstances. And, his beloved, the one with whom he felt safe. The keeper of all of his secrets. The one who loved him unconditionally. It's a wonder he was as good a father as he tried.

And did he do the right thing? Who knows? All I know is what I don't know: what it means to be in fear of losing my freedom or worse yet, my life, because of who I am. Or what it means to be overlooked for jobs or not allowed into clubs, because of my last name. Or how hard it is to find a nice piece of white fish. So perhaps he managed to do what all good fathers set out to do—-protect us.

So what now, I asked myself at 30? Does this new knowledge change who I am? Do I have to start kvetching and shriptzing and getting verklempt? It certainly seemed appealing.

Fast forward 10 years when I was studying sperm donors as my partner and I searched for the father of our child. We immediately fell in love with the author of one application for the position. He was bright and witty and well beyond his 21 years. There were others. Better lookers. More superior physical characteristics. But, this one. This one was special. The last line of his essay sealed it for us.

"I am proud of my heritage. Jews are God's chosen people and I hope you will tell your child how important this is. ...for all those who died before us in the cause."

Another ten years later, I have a wry, witty son with the same red hair as my father. I explain to him the significance of his rich background.

"Mama," he quips, "my father is Jewish so it doesn't count, Oy vey!"

L-R The Boys: Alan, Dad, Frankie, Noel, Mickie, and Petie

"Santa In The Hood"

"Yes, Virginia, there is a Santa Claus."

Everyone remembers that famous line from an editorial written by Francis P. Church in response to a letter to the editor of the New York Sun from a little girl named Virginia O'Hanlon, asking, "Is there a Santa Claus?"

What I don't remember is how old I was when I realized this was just a sweet letter and there really was no Santa Claus. I do know that I pretended to believe long after I stopped buying the story. After all, there was an extra present in it for me. No point in blowing a plum gig when you've got one. With a herd of brothers and sisters hungry to share the wealth of the holidays, every little bit counted.

"Stop shaking the tree, little Judy. There are no more presents!"

I really can't complain because my younger brother, Petie, and I fared better than our older siblings did when they were our age. The level of loot may not compare to today's standards, but then again, what does?

It's amazing how far children will go to believe and how far parents will go to get them to. Growing up in the projects, we received the modified version of old St. Nick coming down the chimney. The closest thing we had to a fireplace was the incinerator just steps from our front door, where everyone on the floor dumped their garbage. It just didn't make sense to have Santa dodging empty tuna cans and milk cartons to deliver the goods. Instead, my mother told us that Santa Claus would shrink himself and slip through our keyhole. The thought of that big tub of lard and that equally stuffed bag o'toys slipping through the cracks was pretty far-fetched, I must say. But, then again, we were raised Catholics and taught that the mother of

Christ was a virgin and water was turned into wine and Jesus arose from the dead, so how difficult would it be to convince us that St. Nick, the patron saint of presents, couldn't pull his own Criss Angel show. So, we bought it.

Every Christmas Eve, my parents would leave Santa a shot of "wodka," as my Hungarian father would say. Santa needed something to help him fight the bitter cold as he flitted throughout the country on that convertible sleigh, you see. And every Christmas morning we awoke to find the empty shot glass and a big smile on Daddy's face. I was 30 before I realized that other kids left cookies and milk.

I recall one year when Petie was just too excited to sleep. "I can hear reindeer hooves and Santa's sleigh bells!" he exclaimed.

I looked out the window to see our drunken neighbors, the Ryans, tromping up the sidewalk, decorated like Christmas trees and three sheets to the wind.

The confusing part was in the weeks prior to Christmas when you'd find Santa Claus on every corner. Pathetic-looking ones at that. Instead of robust, jolly, apple-faced men with shiny white beards, we'd often run into a sack of skin and bones, with straggly gray strands stuck to his chin and the rags of his pants beating him to death.

"They're Santa's helpers," my mother would explain in her thick Irish brogue. "God help us."

When I became a mother, I too, had to have all the answers. Only someone changed the questions. In our particular case, Cory and Shea's grandfather, or Papaw, as they call him, happens to look just like Santa—24-7, 365. And, of course, every Christmas, he dons the suit and plays the part.

"My Papaw is Santa," Cory explained to his wide-eyed pre-school class when he was three. "He's coming for Christmas and staying at my house."

"Santa lives in the North Pole!" one classmate protested

"He lives in Hemet," Cory corrected.

My daughter Shea, who still believes, thinks she has an in with Santa and all she has to do is tell my father-in-law what she wants and voila, it's hers. Instead of waiting in line with the other poor schlubs to sit on that phony Santa's lap, she has the ear of the top man. Not bad.

Things certainly have changed since I was a kid. Oh, and by the way, we will not be leaving Santa vodka as has been the Lane tradition for lo those many years. A nice glass of Kendall Jackson will suit Santa just fine—I'm sure.

JUDY LANE

"My Father the Feminist"

Despite the fact that my parents lived typically conventional lives for a couple who married in the 40s and had children up through the late 50s, my Daddy and Ozzie Nelson had about as much in common as Fred Flintstone and Fred Astaire. For one thing, my father wouldn't be caught dead sipping a frothy drink through a straw at the local malt shop and I don't believe Mr. Nelson ever threw a socket wrench at his son while chasing him down the street screaming Hungarian death threats. But, when it came to a feminine side, the Oz couldn't hold a candle to my Pop.

My father earned a living at the factory all day, while my mother made it all worth living, staying home with the children. Yet, when my father was home, he just as readily changed the diapers as change the TV channels and was always there to lay on the healing hand on our feverish heads, and even cook our meals. I recall one of my father's baking crazes when he pledged to perfect the cheesecake. The words, "light" and "fluffy" had no place in his repertoire, however. He gave "stick to your ribs" and "Mummy, I think he's trying to poison us!" new meaning. With a collection of his creations, my brothers built a fort that lasted well past the Summer of Love.

When my father retired in the '70s, the feminist movement was in full swing and women across America were burning their bras. My father was setting his own little fires in my mother's kitchen, as he had more time than ever to hone his homemaking skills. He soon took to the sewing machine and began hemming and mending like Cinderella on crack. One day, while his cake (and I use the term lightly) cooled on the rack and his head was to the bobbin, a repairperson came to fix the telephone. My mother let the woman in, leading her past

33

my father, who sat at his machine draped in an apron.

"You mean a voman is going to fix de phone?" he asked, eyeing her over the top of his glasses.

"That's funny coming from you, Betsy Ross," the repairwoman quipped.

That afternoon, the two gender pioneers shared a good laugh and a God-awful piece of cake.

Long before it was cool or politically correct or just a way to get on a woman's good side, getting in touch with his feminine side was just another facet to the enigma that was my father. The same man who could freeze you in your tracks with the sound of his thunderous voice or crack a walnut to pieces with his bare hands, could openly weep during those rare moments he spoke of his sisters and their children who perished in the Holocaust. The finger that could extinguish a burning flame could just as easily land like a butterfly on your nose as a demonstration of pure affection. The man who could bend railroad ties in half could shamelessly profess his absolute adoration for our mother on a daily basis.

Lest you get too sappy, let me point out that this was also the father who, upon meeting one of my teenaged suitors for the first time, remarked,

"Vell look at you! You look like thet guy on the TV show Zorro."

"I look like Zorro?" the boy beamed.

"No," my father corrected him. "Sergeant Garcia."

"Summertime and the Livin' is Easy"

Summertime and the livin' is easy. If you're a kid, that is.

All my life, I've lived on one shore or the other. Born and raised in New York, it was the Atlantic, and from high school till today, the Pacific. So, the ultimate red-letter day for us was a trip to the beach. Even more so on the East Coast when the long winters and spring had us aching for the lazy, hazy, crazy days of summer.

Dad, or older siblings, were the route to the beach for most of us. While they took care of all the logistics, your only job was to get into your swimsuit, roll up your towel, and try not to ask, "Are we there yet?"

My father used his precious five days of vacation every year, hauling us to the beach for most of that. This was early immigrant/pre-car days for us. So, this trek involved getting five or six of us to the subway station and out to Coney Island for a trip that took longer to get there than the time we actually spent at the ocean.

Lunch, and I use the term loosely, consisted of hard-boiled eggs and water, or if we were lucky, Kool-Aid. My sister and I shared our eggs since I preferred whites while she the yolks. The great tragedy of the day was when you accidentally dropped your "meal" in the sand. But, with a brush of your hand and a "kiss up to God," the morsel was repaired and quickly gobbled up before one of our brothers could snatch it away.

While the ride there was thrilling and full of anticipation, the return was anything but. Sun burned, wet and bottoms full of sand, we were no doubt enough to make my father question not only the wisdom in doing this at all, but why he didn't just take off with that Parisian model back in '39 instead of marrying my Irish mother and having eight kids with her.

35

JUDY LANE

Despite the hellish experience of our excursions to the beach, the results were the same. We were ecstatic. Our beggar's lunch was our Happy Meal and our red, raw skin allowed us to take the beach back home with us for a while. The smell of Coppertone still conjures up utter joy and anticipation of what this adventure was like. Today is another story.

We head off to the beach with my kids lathered in triple digit SPF, strapped and secured in the backseat like Baccarat crystal pieces being shipped to Greenland, and earphones stuck on their heads so they're too hypnotized to ask, "Are we there yet?" And, they are just as thrilled and just as motivated to get wet, sandy and scratchy as I was. Only, I'm the parent and things aren't looking so peachy from where I sit. Actually, there's not much about a trip to the beach that has me doing cartwheels. On the contrary.

I'm not crazy about any kind of water except perhaps the kind one would use to chase down a shot now and then. Add to it that it's salty and knocks you around like a rag doll and I'm shoutin' whoop-de-flippin-do.

Short of having someone slap me across the puss with a wet rag for a couple of hours, I'm thinking this is probably one of the most annoying activities one could engage in voluntarily. Sand is everywhere and ends up in my teeth, nose and creases and crevices that are simply unnatural. If I wanted to sandpaper my ass, I could have accomplished that quite nicely and with less aggravation in the privacy of my garage. Either way, it's not on my top ten list of things to do before I die.

Within an hour or two, the children get hot and testy and their overwhelming joy rolls out with the ugly, brown tide.

As my children's roadie, I must now lug back all those items I've hauled in—toys, food, change of clothes, chairs, towels, umbrellas, puppies, lizards, trophies and anything else that we just can't do without for a couple of hours away from home.

I'm beginning to wonder. What exactly did my father bring to the beach? A tisket a tasket, those eggs fit in one basket. And, there were certainly no chairs for sitting or toys for playing—that's what brothers are for. The same towel that wiped us dry served as our beach blanket—and napkin. The only sunscreen we had was when my father stood in front of us.

I think my father was on to something. Yes, he had to haul us a long way for a brief respite, but at what cost? Half of us were instructed to "run undah the turnstile and don't look bek!" Our mother made the meal. And as far as our fighting and whining all the way home, conveniently he was deaf in one ear.

The one who truly benefited was my mother. She got to have the apartment to herself for a few hours a day and probably laughed herself silly at the thought of my father leading the troops into battle and back again.

So, as I sit in my chair, toes in the sand, watching the sun slowly dipping into the ocean, I look over at Pepper, who is quite stunning in the reddish glow, breathe in the fresh, salty air and sigh, "We are never leaving home without a thermos of Margaritas again!"

JUDY LANE

"You Talkin' To Me?"

My father was virtually deaf in one ear, a fact that he learned to not only live with, but also use to his advantage.

"Daddy, can I have my allowance?"

"Vot? I kent hear you?" he would shout in his thick Hungarian accent, cupping his good ear.

"Daddy, there's Nathan's! Let's stop for franks!"

"Eh? Did zombudy zay zomzing?" he'd replied as he pressed the gas pedal harder.

It was also the thing that made him funny and charming to the rest of the world.

"Don't forget your cash, Mr. Lane," said the bank teller.

"Vot? Hesh? No I don't eat hesh. Thenk you anyvey," he would quip.

And especially with the pretty young women.

"Is that frozen or fresh?" the cutie beyond the counter at the fish market asked him?

"Vot? You vont to get fresh wit me? Okay, but hurry before my vife comes."

"Oh, Mr. Lane..." she'd smile and blush.

But, just try to whisper to your sister about what a "crazy, frustrating nutcase" he was on any particular day. The CIA had nothing on him.

"I ken hear you!" he'd shout from across the street, adjusting his built-in big ear.

While his deaf ear was flat up against his head, his "good ear" was permanently stuck out. We assumed it was from years of cupping and pointing it like radar in the direction of his intended surveillance. This, of course, earned him a secret nickname among us kids—-The Cup.

"I heard that!" he'd scream.

While my mother would violently shake her newspaper as a warning when we were getting on her last and final nerve, my father would sit quietly reading amidst the constant chaos that was home.

"Let dey play," he would say quietly to my mother.

I'm sure she wanted to hit him upside the head with her teapot. But, she didn't. She adored The Cup.

I recall once when I was about 5 and had done an evil deed of some kind. I decided to fess up to my father since I thought he might understand this particular issue much better than my mother. It was difficult to get "quality time" with seven brothers and sisters mulling around like gazelles at the watering hole.

"What's goin' on? What's the matta wit her?"

So, I decided to sidle up next to him. I grabbed hold of his head and whispered my confession in his ear. When I was done, I felt a huge sense of relief, particularly when I noticed that he was smiling. It's all good, I thought. I'm in the clear. I won't have to deal with Mummy—he'll do that. Whew. I scampered away, happy as a little clam. It wasn't until years later that I realized that I was talking in the deaf ear.

Fortunately, both of my ears are perfectly healthy. In fact, I score somewhere up there with cocker spaniels on hearing tests. But, I, too, possess the ability to tune out. When I was a child, it was a survival mechanism. It was the only way to get homework done at the kitchen table in an apartment with nine other people talking and laughing and otherwise carrying on at decibel levels somewhere between vacuum cleaner and jet engine.

And, now as a mother of two equally noisy children, I am able to tune them out in order to read a book, watch a TV program or do a crossword puzzle. All while Pepper is shaking her paper violently as a final warning. When that fails, she becomes the referee who has just pulled Mike Tyson off Evander Holyfield's ear. At last, she has banished them to their respective corners, cleaned up the mess and slumps into her chair in a heap.

"Did somebody say something?" I finally ask.

She probably wants to hit me upside the head with my teapot. But, she doesn't. She adores me. That's what I hear anyway.

Mummy & Daddy on the Queen Mary, 1949

JUDY LANE

COME TO MAMA

JUDY LANE

"Mourning Sickness"

Why didn't anyone tell me about this? My sisters. My niece. My friends. I've heard people talk about "morning sickness." Now wouldn't you assume that means between, oh say, 7:00 a.m. and 12 Noon? Not!

Maybe it's really "mourning sickness," and somebody mixed it up a long time ago and we all just assumed it was "morning sickness." Like a "White" Rhino. Everybody assumes it's a "White Rhino," but it's not. It's a "wide" Rhino. I saw it on the Discovery Channel. The Dutch were actually describing its wide lips not its white color--since it's really gray, anyway. Where was I? Oh, yeah. Morning, Noon and Night Sickness.

Nobody told me it was gonna be like this. I finally asked my fellow women.

"So, did you have morning sickness?"

"What morning?! I had it all day!"

I didn't' know this. Where was I?

I've decided that you are not told certain things until you belong to the club. You see, there's a general club that all women belong to by virtue of the fact that they have those two X chromosomes. We acknowledge one another when we meet. We nod knowingly when even a stranger says something negative about her man. We assume she's right and he's wrong. We are in the Women's Club.

What I've discovered is that there are chapters in the Club--just like a big Alumni Association. There's the general alumni association for everyone who graduated from a particular school. Then, there are smaller clubs or chapters for those who graduated and live in Arizona, or those who graduated and are Republicans, or Latino or whatever.

JUDY LANE

The Women's Club and its Chapters don't advertise for members. When, and if, you meet the criteria you'll be contacted by other women and automatically ushered into the club. No information about the club or its members is made available to you until you are an official member. Members of the Club and it's Chapters do socialize, work and even cohabitate with non-club members. But, they operate under different criteria when they are outside the club. Try as they might, men are never privy to what really goes on inside the club. They can visit. They can even participate. But they are merely guests. They are not members.

There is only one dues structure--lifetime. You pay your dues and become a life member. Some women pay more dues than others, and some pay their dues over and over again. But what makes up the dues is the same for everyone--suffering. Those who have paid
higher dues usually rise to some official status in the club, or at least, are revered by the other members.

When I became pregnant, I automatically became a member of a Chapter. Right now it's the Pregnancy Chapter. It's not quite the Mother's Chapter--I haven't paid my dues yet. But I'm definitely in the Pregnancy Chapter--I'm sick, bloated, emotional, scared, excited, dizzy and actively losing brain cells. I'm now a life member of the Pregnancy Chapter.

Meetings occur everywhere and anywhere. No need for notices or agendas. They just happen. In restaurants, hotel lobbies and even in elevators. The most common meeting place is in the waiting room at the OB/GYN. This is where you hear things that are written nowhere. Not in the Bible or even "What To Expect When You're Expecting."

I still feel sick all the time, but it is comforting to know I'm not going to die. I may become an officer in the club but I'm really not going to die.

JUDY LANE

"I Know Why A Caged Cow Moos"

Whenever a book touts itself as the "...authority" or the "...most comprehensive" on any topic, you can bet there are more missing parts than a jigsaw puzzle at a rummage sale.

When I was pregnant I was inundated with literature on "everything" I needed to know about pregnancy. Except, of course, all the things that happened to me.

Then, I was showered with baby books that claim to predict everything that my little one, Cory Peter, was going to do. Except, of course--well, you get the idea.

I studied up on breast-feeding to ensure I could give my little guy the best possible start in life. I had all the moves down pat. I was schooled on "what to expect..." Except, for <u>that</u> move. The one Cory did about half way through his feeding. He'd latch on just fine, staring up at me with that look of total contentment--just like they say in the book. Then suddenly he'd shake his head back and forth and tug at my breast like it was a dog's chew toy.

"Grrrr!" he'd coo as he stretched me out like a piece of salt water taffy. Then, he jerked his head back and comes up for air like a pirate swilling rum.

"Aye, matey--er, I mean Mama. Got milk?"

A mammogram had nothing on Cory. In one month, I went from a 40D to a 40 long.

What happened to the "quiet moment between your baby and you."? The "serenity and peace you will experience"? I guess no one's ever given birth to Tarzan's Boy.

Pepper helped with Cory's 2 a.m. feeding. While I got some sleep, he was fed from a bottle in another room. Although I'm sure Cory could probably have pulled my breast down the hallway like one of those air pump hoses at the gas station. When he was done, he could just let go and watch it shoot back into place. Snap!

That feeding break was a great comfort to me. Except that by morning, I was pumped up to feed--if you know what I mean.

One morning, I awoke with a start at 6 a.m. I heard that familiar tiny peep come from the next room. I rushed out to find Pepper cradling Cory with a big, fat bottle hanging out of his mouth.

"I thought I'd let you sleep," she beamed.

I stood there agape, feeling like one of Austin Powers' Fembots with my Jayne Mansfield bumpers ready to fire.

"What am I supposed to do with these?" I screamed.

It was at that moment I understood why cows moo.

A few minutes later I was hooked up to a contraption that looked like a reject from an S&M catalog. It's called a breast pump. Industrial strength. It's made for today's woman. The booklet shows an executive dressed in a business suit, high-heeled shoes, hair in a bun--the works. She's busy on the phone while pumping milk for her child who's being cared for elsewhere. This kind of liberation I can do without.

I guess I'll just have to find out all the important stuff for myself. 'Cause I searched through my stacks and didn't find one single chapter on how a tiny wail that sounds amazingly just like "Mama" can turn a grown woman into putty, ready to hand over the checkbook and the car keys to a two-month old.

My experience had far-reaching effects as well. You see, I'm not much of an advocate. About anything. Voting and eating hot dogs on July 4th is as political as I get. But, like most people it takes a personal experience to propel me to action.

Several years ago when I broke my ankle and found myself on crutches for six weeks, I became painfully aware of the obstacles those with disabilities face. As a pregnant woman, I was ready to march to Washington to get more public restrooms built in my city. And then, as a nursing mother, I was once again poised to duke it out with somebody.

America is not ready for a woman to breast-feed her child in public. San Francisco recently passed an ordinance that it is okay for a woman to breast-feed in public--so long as a child is involved, of course. That's like proclaiming it's all right to eat popcorn at the movies.

Bosoms are splashed all over the screens--big and small--the screens, that is. They cover magazines--men's and women's. They sell everything from toothpaste to toilet bowl cleaners. Sometimes even bras. And suddenly, we need law makers to sanction their originally intended use.

I've never been completely at ease baring certain body parts. In high school, I claimed to be from a little known, extremely conservative religious sect so I wouldn't have to shower for gym. It hasn't gotten much better as I've gotten older. I suspect this is in direct correlation to the noticeable deterioration of said parts. In any case, I only breast-fed in public because I was forced to. I'm not crazy about exposing myself before God and my country.

There are very few public facilities that offer women a suitable place for handling this. I was shopping with Pepper at Macy's. At the San Francisco store no less. Within seconds Cory Peter went from "goo-goo, ga-ga" to "Feed me!!" Like Audrey, the insatiable man-eating plant from Little Shop of Horrors, my little angel became quite persistent about his

51

immediate need.

"The ladies room is on the third floor," said Pepper as I grabbed the baby, who was now in the stiff, "I'm-holding-my-breath-and-turning-blue stage." We were on the eighth floor.

"Take the escalator!" Pepper yelled. "It'll be much faster than the elevator.

Famous last words. Like siren whaling through a war-torn city, Cory made his point more clearly to me and everyone else on what seemed to be the biggest shopping day next to Christmas Eve as I rushed to the escalators.

It was obviously tourist season as the group in front of me stood frozen and gawking at every floor. The concept of the moving stair escaped these out-of-towners as we all bunched up like fallen dominoes at each landing. All the while, Cory is reaching new decibels in his quest for immediate gratification.

At the sixth floor I spotted the bedding department. What better place for a quiet moment for mother and son? I soon lay relaxing on one of those faux beds (did you know that they are not regulation size?) providing my son with the nourishment he needed. Cory lay smugly up against me lapping up lunch as stunned semi-annual, white sale shoppers thought they had stumbled upon a Candid Camera episode.

It turned out that the one and only ladies room had (a) toilets, (b) sinks; and of course, (c) a line of women waiting. But, no place to sit down much less to feed a baby. So what's a mother to do but take matters into her own hands--or whatever.

On one of our road trips, I sat in the backseat with my little treasure while Pepper drove. We were one hour from our destination on a desolate road with no rest areas. No exits, no shoulders, no nothin'. Cory had sucked down his rations for the

five-hour trip and was now demanding "More! More! More!"
I threw caution, and any shred of dignity that survived labor, to
the wind. I unbuckled my seat belt and my nursing bra,
straddled Cory's car seat and proceeded to give new meaning to
the word "fast food."

I'm sure there's a trucker somewhere with one of those
"Show me your tits" signs who got more than he bargained for.

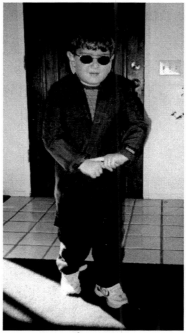

The Boy

JUDY LANE

"Whosiwhatsit"

When Cory was three, I was getting him dressed one morning like every other morning. He wanted to watch Big Comfy Couch. I wanted to watch the news. I'm bigger so I won.

Who knows what channel? It really doesn't matter. It was one of those generic morning programs. You know, with the attractive male and female anchor and a heavyset, jovial weatherman. This day, they were interviewing a psychologist who was discussing the importance of teaching your children the proper names for body parts.

"A teachable moment," she explained, "could be when you see a pregnant woman. You could say, 'in a special place inside her uterus, a baby is being created,'" she said.

I almost choked on my cruller. I couldn't even cover Cory's ears because I was too busy covering mine.

"When you're teaching your child other body parts," she continued, "you could merely say, 'This is your nose, this is your mouth, this is your tummy and this is your vulva.'"

I rushed into the bathroom to get a cold compress. I'm just not ready for this, I thought. I was 25 and married for four years before I realized that vulva wasn't a Swedish import.

I realized that I was going to have to handle this at some point. Like most three-year olds, Cory had already discovered his joystick and it wouldn't be long before he starts asking, "What's this?"

But, why exactly must we be so formal? If we can say tummy instead of abdomen, why can't I say wienie instead of the "P" word?

I long for the good-old days when men were men and their equipment was the family jewels. Besides, no matter what

I told Cory, like most men, he's going to eventually give it a nickname anyway. A former sweetheart of mine called his "Big Thunder." I renamed it "Light Drizzle," but that's another story.

I'm an old broad and can't bring myself to use the "proper" names for my body parts.

"I have a pain, well, uh, down there," I say to the doctor.

"Under the table?" she says as she goes searching for my problem.

"A little higher," I respond sheepishly.

A friend of mine is big into the appropriate name business. Her children sound like pre-med students as the "V" and "P" words roll off their tongues. But to my friend's chagrin, one of her children yelled out at the top of her lungs in the middle of the grocery store,"

"My vagina hurts!"

That would be enough to send me and the child into solitary confinement for the next 15 years.

It's all Ken Starr's fault. His report had that "p" word thrown around like confetti. I couldn't turn on the TV without hearing about the President's whosiwhatsit.

Perhaps when Cory's old enough, say 30, we can work this out. By then, I'll be senile and won't remember my own name much less the appropriate names for body parts. Until then, I'm going to continue to cover my ta-tas and hoo-ha when he comes into my bedroom and will try not to shriek when I catch him playing with his thingamajig.

JUDY LANE

"Puppy Love"

Why I needed to add another dog to our family when I already have one huge Newfoundland, Bear, one pretty good-size 10-year old boy, Cory, and one feisty seven-year old girl, Shea, is beyond me. So, I'll spare you the back story and get to the part where we begin the search for a used pooch.

Everywhere you turn, there are horror stories about the thousands of dogs euthanized every year because they can't find good homes for them. Well, here we were ready and willing to do our part, so how hard could it be? I suspect Angelina Jolie had an easier time adopting than I did.

First, they send you profiles of all the candidates. Naturally, my daughter falls in love with every one that comes across the screen.

"I want April!" Shea squealed as she eyed one scrawny, hairless little thing.

"Are you sure that's a dog, Shea?" I asked. "I think it's a rat."

"Oh, look at Trixie! I love her! Oh, wait, look at Sprinkles!"

And, so it went. But, I soon found out that a willingness to disrupt one's home and a desperate little girl are not enough for these pet rescue types. They want real commitment.

"You'll need to fill out this application before you can see any dog," the rescue worker snaps.

"Isn't time of the essence?" I quip, with images of all those poor mongrels headed for the big dog park in the sky.

"We take this very seriously. Fill out the application. Then we'll talk."

After providing DOB's SSN's, GPS, bra sizes and blood types for anyone who's ever crossed your threshold, you get to be interviewed over the phone.

"Do you realize that adopting a dog is a full-time commitment? That you must feed them, walk them, bathe them, and care for them in sickness and in health?"

I quickly hung up, beads of sweat on my forehead, afraid that if I answered "I do," I'd be married to a Great Dane and living on a farm in Nebraska or something.

But, with my daughter pressuring me, I persevered. Finally, we were granted an audience.

"I love Bubbles!" Shea squealed when she set eyes on a three-legged dog.

"But, honey, she's, well, she's handicapped."

"Aaaaaaannnnd?" she said eyeing me.

"Aaaaaaannnnd, that's great," I replied. "We'll take her!"

"Not so fast, sister," said the handler. Well, maybe she didn't call me "sister," but it felt that way. "We'll need to think about this."

We'll need to think about this? Wasn't this dog snatched off the chopping block just days earlier? Maybe somebody should ask Bubbles.

"We don't think Bubbles is the right fit for your family," the handler stated in a cold, harsh telephone message.

Now, I'm beginning to have a complex. Adopting Shea was a piece cake compared to this.

Weeks pass as Shea continues to fall in love with every click of the mouse. Agatha, Harley, Darla and Jellybean. Foxy, Lucy, Ollie and Guapo. She loves them all. And, again, we are told to "go home and think about it."

Finally, the day comes. We're so elated that we were "almost fully approved," to adopt, Sophie, a 2-year old purebred Cocker Spaniel that I forgot about the $150 I have to pay for the privilege, that I must drive 3-1/2 hours one way just to meet the dog, and that they still must determined if "there's a relationship there." I draw the line on stuffing my miniature horse in the back of the car for a half-day ride just to allow the "two dogs to bond."

Despite the fact that the rescue lady now has my entire life story, including ex-husbands and minor brushes with the law, she somehow fails to reveal a few particulars herself until my daughter is stuck on Sophie like a frat boy on his kegger.

"Hmm," I say, as I eye the 'Cocker Spaniel,' "She looks like she might be mixed with something."

"Oh, you think so?" the foster mom mumbles, avoiding eye contact. "You never know what these dogs do."

"She seems very mellow," I remark as Sophie remains fixed in one spot like a little mop posted in the corner.

"Oh, yes, well we just had her spayed. But, it's all fine. Just take her to the vet next week and have the stitches removed. Most vets do that for free."

And exactly what vet is she talking about? The guy from World War II? Because there ain't no dog doctor that's ever done anything for one of my dogs for free.

"And, that's $150, right?" I say as I begin to write the check.

"Actually, it's $200," she corrects me.

Of course. I fully expected her to add "...and because your front door faces East instead of West, which is very bad for alleged Cocker Spaniels, that'll be an extra $100."

But, what could I do? My daughter was beaming like she just, well, just got the dog of her dreams. And, whatever Sophie is or isn't, she sure is cute. I just had one final question.

"She's housebroken, right?" I say.

"Oh, yes...95%."

Well, the 5% peed and crapped all over my carpet the minute I set her down at home.

But, when my Bear took a look at Sophie and looked up at me with what I can only describe as a smile, I knew we were meant to be. Forsaking all others, till death, well, you know.

"Not Guilty By Reason of Menopausanity"

When your family threatens to commit you—-that or stab you to death with a fork in your sleep, maybe it's time to seek professional help. And, so I did. With a pen and paper in hand and "Menopause" written at the top of the page, I began my journey to get back to me.

I flipped through the Yellow Pages, bodysurfed the Internet and kept watch for a TV commercial that addressed my problem. As an aside, it's clear that if you have erectile dysfunction, feminine itching or things that are unspeakable and only alluded to in the ads (although I'm not sure what's left), the dinner hour is the optimum time for everyone from little three-year old Ashleigh up to Great Granny Flo, seated together, chomping on ribs and cornbread, to get the information you need. But, if you're like me, you find no consolation and just another reason to throw your squatty shoe at the TV, prompting the family to form that familiar little huddle and then demand that you "do something!"

I was determined to prove my theory and present a paper to the AMA and U.S. Congress that menopausal women could do more damage in Iraq than all the allied troops combined. When the sound of your kid chewing gum causes you to shriek at jet engine-decibel-levels and to threaten to box them up and give them away along with the clothes you have set out for the Salvation Army, you can imagine what a threat from the armed enemy would conjure up. But, alas, you're an army of one and obviously must tone it down a little in order to stay out of jail and live harmoniously with your fellow Americans despite the fact that everyone is stupid and nobody can do anything right! Deep breath.

JUDY LANE

Before you could say "bone loss," I found myself sitting across from a doctor sharing my woes. Pepper was at my side, more to ensure that I didn't run out of the joint than to provide support, I suspect. Like an eager drama student, she felt the need to embellish everything I reported.

"I'm a little cranky," turned into "She's like a junkyard dog that hasn't been fed in four days." "I may be a tad impatient with the kids," was soon "The children have taken to calling her Tsumomi." "People seem to be getting on my nerves," became "The Neighborhood Watch Group has Judy's picture plastered on lamp posts and store fronts throughout the city."

Reluctantly, I agreed to a regimen of unnatural chemicals. The doctor couldn't guarantee the results and felt that it would be a long process since it takes time to get the right balance of drugs.

"You'll have to do a little experimentation," she said.

The last time I experimented with drugs, I saw my unborn children in the eyes of a shiftless, longhaired boy in a Nehru jacket and bell-bottoms offering me a life on the road in his dilapidated VW bus. Luckily, an image of my father's face suddenly flashed in the idyllic picture and I ran two miles home to sleep it off.

The first couple of weeks on my new drug regimen were not much different. Although I did seem to be a little more controlled. While I still fantasized about poking certain people in the eye and running other drivers off the road, I did stop lunging at least. Then, I began to experience unpleasant symptoms.

"I'm nauseated, lightheaded, dizzy and bloated," I said on the message I left for my doctor, who told me to call her any time day or night.

A week later, I got a return message.

"Yes, I'm looking for Judy Enal. If this is her number, please call me." I figured she was a comedian, like me. The enal was Lane spelled backwards and she was just being funny...right? Then, another message followed.

"Uh, yes, Judy, well, um I checked with several docs around here they all agreed that the symptoms you described are not related to the drugs I gave you. Call me if you need anything else."

In doing my bi-annual car cleaning, I found, stuck to the floorboard, covered in Juicy Juice and marked in crayons, the insert they include with prescriptions drugs. There in black and white was a list of six "typical symptoms," five of which I described to the doctor. I couldn't help but wonder who were these "docs" she polled. Doc Severson, the musical conductor? Doc Holiday, the TB-riddled gunslinger/medicine man? Happy and Grumpy's older brother? I could just see her strolling through the hospital poking her head into the gift shop.

"Hey volunteer, I need to ask you something."
And supply closets...

"You! You with the broom..."

The sixth symptom, "lack of sexual drive," is laughable. It's hard to feel like making out when you're bloated like the Michelin Man and crumpled like a used bean bag on the bathroom floor, head on the throne because you're just not sure where this nausea is going. And you can just imagine your sweetheart getting hot and heavy over someone who is screaming out the window at other drivers, "I'm not only going to kill you, I'm going to kill everyone you ever met!"

The doctors seemed to be a little biased about their way to handle my problem. Never once did they recommend a change in diet or a healthy supplement that I could find at Trader Joe's or something. I just couldn't be sure if they were being objective in their recommendations, I thought to myself as I scanned the doctor's office filled with clocks, calendars, note pads and desk blotters with logos of all the drugs they were prescribing.

"I'll walk out with you," she said, putting on her Provera™ raincoat and carrying her Estrace™ umbrella.

My own research on the Internet netted me a date with someone in Bulgaria, cream to enlarge my penis and much of the inheritance of a very kind, but misunderstood prince in Nigeria, but not much on what I was going through. All the self-help, mother earth-type websites revealed that this was a drug-company conspiracy and that I needed to free myself of the chains that bind me—in more ways than one. Millet, oat bran cakes and soy would replace my coffee, Merlot and chocolate diet. I decided I'd rather go insane.

Pharmaceutical websites stood behind their products, assuring me that these were just random cases of severe side effects despite what I see on Law and Order each week. Besides, they had done serious testing to determine if the drugs were safe for chubby, 50-ish women.

"It has been determined that prolonged use of this drug has caused breast cancer in Beagles," said one article.

Like everything else, I'm going to just have to find my own way. No doubt my family will keep me posted on how I'm doing.

And, if I start barking and scratching and drinking out of the toilet, well maybe we'll need to pursue this a little more.

JUDY LANE

"Girls Just Wanna Have Fun"

There probably isn't a parent alive who, while witnessing their little angel holding a magnifying glass over an ant, doesn't wonder, "Is this one of the warning signs of a budding sociopath?"

Cory went from diapers to smoking jacket. He asked me if it would be all right to host weekly "discussion groups" at our house with his boys when he was 7. I couldn't imagine his buddies standing in one place for more than a minute much less swapping ideas around a table for an hour, but rather than burst his bubble, I sat down with him and mapped out some topics: "Who's the best superhero?" "How to keep your little sister from touching your stuff," "Favorite desserts."

Shea is another story. As a toddler, she was the poster child for "101 ways a child can off themselves if left unattended for more than a minute."

I'm not sure where to start. Was it the time she was sitting on the couch watching TV and casually put a plastic bag over her head? Or when she mouthed the exhaust pipe on our SUV? Or maybe the time, after reading to her the warning on a box she was pointing to, "Danger High Voltage! Stand Back! Don't Touch. No, really," and she put one tiny finger on it. Or when she looked me straight in the eye as I warned her that the burner on the stove was hot and then placed her full hand square on the glowing ring.

Shea is a kind of see-for-myself gal. I could tell her that electrical outlets are dangerous, but she still had the need to stick a screwdriver in there...while standing in a bowl of water...balancing a steak knife on her nose...and unscrewing the Drano. The subsequent curly hair worked but the charred

face and hands were not pretty. If a cat has nine lives, Shea is
Felix the Cat reincarnated.

I figure she was probably just testing us with these
pranks. But, I became a little more concerned about other
behavior.

"Why exactly did you put glue in the dog's ear?"

That has been followed with, "...pull the dog's fur out?"
"...wrap your purse straps around the dog's throat?" "...lock the
dog in the bathroom?" and "...put a jellybean up the dog's
nose."

Her typical response was a widening of her already
saucer-like eyes and a shrug of her shoulders. If this were a
cartoon strip, there would be a bubble over her head reading,
"seemed like a good idea at the time."

Like all good, sane, intelligent parents, we alternately
cursed, screamed, threatened bodily harm and ultimately
removed items one-by-one from her room. This worked so well.
With just four walls and bed in her once cluttered room, she
still managed to get into trouble.

"Why exactly did you smear shaving cream all over the
carpet?"

When she wasn't racing through a kitchen restaurant
checking out the butcher knives, she was winking and lowering
her chocolate eyes, flirting shamelessly with the waiters and bus
boys.

"Ooooh. I want to marry him," she exclaimed when a
motorcyclist sped by our car.

"Pepper," I asked one morning picking up Shea pooh
along with the dog's in the backyard, "do you suppose there's
anything seriously wrong?"

"She did tell me she was going to cut off my head the other day," Pepper replied. "But I'm sure it's just kid's stuff.

"Yea, that's what Mrs. Menendez said," I replied.

Then it came. The pre-school "Student Progress Report." She was scored on a scale of one to four for things like listening and speaking; writing, math and reading, and social-emotional development.

"Exhibits impulse control and self-regulation—4"

"Responds to adult supervision—4"

"Respects the property of self and others—4"

"Takes care of toileting needs (apparently indoors at school)—4,

"Can hop on one foot-4" and on and on.

All fours.

So, maybe we worried for nothing. We must be doing something right, we thought. So we continued to praise and reward when all was well and took away items when she was pulling her usual stunts.

"I'm giving that to Venla," Pepper threatened her one day, tossing yet another item into that imaginary box of possessions that were to be taken from Shea and given to another, better-behaved child.

This method worked like a charm.

A few weeks later on a stormy morning, I put a hat and rain slicker on her. She stood stiff and angry in the doorway. It was clear she was not thrilled with my fashion sense.

"I have an idea," she said unbuttoning the coat and tossing the hat. "Let's go ahead and give this to Venla."

That's her. My "smart, funny, imaginative child with a strong sense of self."

JUDY LANE

"What To Expect When You're Expecting To Travel"

There's a book called, "100 Things to Do Before You Die." Reading it is on my list of things to do before I die. In the meantime, we traveled to Europe for the first time. At 53, I think this is pretty amazing. Although being able to bend over and tie my shoe at 53 is equally remarkable in my world.

I got a lot of "you've never been out of the country?" comments and I blushed and said, "No." Unless you count Mexico, which if you live in San Diego, you can probably accomplish unwittingly on a drinking binge any given Friday night. So, "No, I've never been out of the country!" I freely admitted. But, that would soon change.

Like first time-parents, Pepper and I read all the books, bought all the accoutrements, consulted the Internet, and asked friends and strangers alike what to expect when expecting to travel overseas. And when we landed in London, we were thoroughly prepared and intact. We navigated through all the Stations of the Cross at the airport and didn't even lose one piece of luggage. Our son, yes. But, luggage no. Oh, yes, that.

There was that one bump in the road. The one thing no one mentioned. Just like when I was pregnant and found myself on the floor unable to get up, spinning and spinning and hoping somehow centrifugal force or some kind of physics would set me upright. In between orbits, I began to count off the days to my delivery and realized nine months equal 10 months in real time, and that they had all lied to me. But, I digress.

No one mentioned one piece of information about the Tube.

We proudly mapped our way from Heathrow airport to the hotel at which we would be spending one night before we hopped another plane to Dublin. Just one stop away on the Tube. No taxis, for us. No, sir. We bravely trekked like all those other people loaded down like mules as we boarded the train. The doors opened and we plodded on. We noticed all the bags piled up against the doors on the other side. And, so we heaped ours on, clutching our children closely to us in the process. The doors remained open unusually long, seemingly waiting for that last minute traveler to board. And, several did.

With just one stop for us, we remained standing. Our pockets full of pounds and Euros, proud of ourselves for managing all this and not once threatening to kill either child. We blushed with internal satisfaction.

It was only minutes as I scanned the collection of riders. It was simply fascinating. Different colors, myriad languages, and yet Universal tones of laughter filled the car as they engaged one another. My eyes paused on one young couple in particular. They were in their early 20s and spoke in a language I couldn't place. He had a beautiful smile and huge brown eyes that laughed as he regaled her with some story. She was simply stunning--and the size of a hood ornament. What a lovely couple, I thought to myself.

As we approached our stop, we alerted the children and began to clutch our heavy bags in preparation to disembark. We faced the doors, plotting our successful exit. As the train slowed to a stop, there it was. That unexpected little thing. No book, no map, no amount of discussion with seasoned travelers touched on this one. The train stopped and the doors we faced remained closed. And, why not? We were facing a brick wall.

But, oh, how they opened behind us. Behind us, where the impromptu luggage department was. We spun around and began to make a path between the heavy bags to find a way out. I pushed aside steamer trunks, as I maneuvered my own gear through the maze.

"Cory!" I called to my big, strong son. "Go out the door, and I'll hand you our stuff."

And, so he did. Waiting in his place like a volunteer firefighter, hands outstretched for the first bucket of water. Instead, the doors promptly closed. The doors that remained open for what seemed like an eternity when we got on earlier. Now, suddenly, it was all chop-chop, time to go.

And now, time stood still. There was my nine-year old son standing outside the train with the Macaulay Culkin face of absolute terror as he realizes what's happening. And, his Moms and little sister, Shea, inside with the luggage and the contingent from the United Nations.

Suddenly, I heard a loud shrieking, which I assumed was either an air raid alarm or an unfortunate cat that got caught on the third rail. Alas, it was my darling, Pepper.

"My boy!" she shrieked.

And like a Superhero sans cape, the charming brown-eyed stranger shot up from his seat and ran to her side.

"Don't worry," he said in his thick accent, "He'll be fine."

While she explained to him the horrors of a "little boy" stranded in London, I caught Cory's eyes and, putting on my best everything-is-fine smile, I mouthed, "Don't worry, we'll be right back to get you. Stay right there."

The look of horror disappeared into the sweet boy smile I know. He waved back to me as the train left the station.

The handsome young stranger convinced her that while this was certainly an emergency for us, it wasn't worthy of pressing the emergency button, that would stop all trains on the continent and alert every fighter pilot between here and Greenland.

She sobbed. I was doing my "just remain calm, just remain calm," mantra, and Shea was, well, Shea.

"Don't worry, Mom," she said to Pepper. "He's nine. He knows all the details."

Later when we asked "what details?" She replied, "You know, 'stop, drop and roll.'"

At the next stop, the young man and his diminutive lady friend, swept up our bags as they guided us off one train and onto the next to where my son sat calmly on a bench. We all rushed him with hugs and kisses and pats on the back—including the young couple. Cory was equally relieved and puzzled as to why these strangers were showering him with affection. But, he's used to the unusual with his Moms, not to mention he wasn't going to argue with a beautiful young woman kissing him on both cheeks.

We bid farewell to our new friends and headed to our hotel, with a death-grip on both children.

"I forgot to ask where they were from?" Pepper said

"They were Turkish," I replied, having had a short conversation with the man who was doing everything to calm our fears.

Then we all remembered another recent encounter with a foreign man.

While driving home one Saturday afternoon, we spotted an elderly gentleman carrying grocery bags and staggering along the sidewalk. We pulled over to see if he was okay.

From his demeanor and fragrance, we determined he had a few too many at the local tavern and so we offered him a ride home. Much to the horror of our children.

"You said 'Never talk to strangers!' 'Never pick up hitchhikers!' What are you doing?!" they shrieked.

While chatting, it was clear he was a recent immigrant. As he climbed out of the car at his driveway, he turned to us and said, "You are the nicest Americans I've ever met. I've been here for five years, and no American has been so nice to me. Bless you both."

"Where are you from?" Pepper called out to him.

"I'm Turkish," he replied.

JUDY LANE

"A Boy's Life"

A mother expects that at some point she'll be in her son's room, minding her own business and casually come across a risqué magazine that he has carefully hidden deep within the heavy mattress and box spring. Or, God forbid, a female's unmentionables. Or, get-my-nitroglycerine-tablets! the female herself. But, I certainly didn't expect it in first grade.

Cory was a typical six-year old boy. On the surface, he had no interest in the opposite sex. And, as a matter of fact, reacted strongly even at the mere mention of the girls in his class.

"They're not my girlfriends! They're friends and they're girls."

And even more strongly when given anything that could be remotely considered, "girly." These included, but were not limited to, anything pink or purple--from a piece of his favorite candy to plastic utensils; floral prints; and movies or TV shows that include dancing and/or kissing.

And yet, I saw his big, caramel eyes widen and literally spin around in their sockets when a Victoria's secret ad was conveniently broadcast during the "family hour." In person at the pool? Well, I have completely lost him and couldn't get his attention if I instantaneously combusted on my chaise lounge.

One evening he asked to speak to me in private. Something was bothering him and he had "to let it out!" I sat him down on the darkened stairway in our home.

"You can tell me anything," I said calmly, all the while thinking, please, please don't go shockin' your Mama.

He squirmed and twisted and agonized while I continued to encourage him to tell me.

Finally, he asked if I recalled a Bernie Mac episode that we watched together some weeks back.

"You know," he said, sheepishly, "the one where the kid kept thinking about--you know."

The episode came flooding back to me. Bernie's flamboyant sister came for a visit, wearing size XS on an XL bust. The young boy was mesmerized by her bodacious tat-tatties and was unable to think of anything else for weeks. Even the Jell-O mold took on female properties.

"That's me," he said, moaning and rubbing his face in his hands. "Mama, I can't think of anything else. Day and night. Night and day!"

"Oh, sweetie," I said, trying not to laugh. "It's okay. That's normal. Nature made woman beautiful so men would be attracted to them, and well, never mind. Let's just leave it at that."

"But, Mama," he continued. "It's worse than that. I did something reeeeeeeally, reeeeeeeally bad."

I knew it. Here I thought I was Clair Huxtable and we could go have some puddin' now, but he was going to drop the bomb.

"I drew a picture and gave it to Spencer" he confessed. "Ooooooh. It was really bad."

"A picture of what?" I asked; doing what every lawyer tells you not to do—don't ask a question if you don't already know the answer.

"A woman with…boobies," he whispered.

"Was she being shot or stabbed or blown up or anything?"

"Huh?" he said, whipping his head up at me as though I had asked if he gargled with lye.

"Just a picture of a woman and her, well, breasts?" I confirmed.

"Mom!" he shrieked.

I explained that it was perfectly fine. As long as no one was getting hurt, it was actually art.

"It's worse than that," he continued.

Lord have mercy! What now? I was wringing my hands and rubbing my face. What could it be? I could see myself Googling "Deviant Behavior in sweet, red-haired, six-year old boys."

"Spencer's mother found it!" he said. "And she ripped it up and screamed at me and said she was going to tell you!" he added, sobbing.

Note to self: Kick Spencer's mother's ass.

"Honey," I assured him. "You did nothing wrong. It's perfectly natural for boys to do that. Your only mistake was giving it to Spencer. From now on, keep that stuff to yourself."

"But what am I going to do?" he asked, drying his tears. "I can't concentrate. Why? Why? Why did nature make them so beautiful?"

I hugged my little man on the stairs and tried to explain that it was just the beginning. He was going to be distracted by these and other equally luscious body parts for the rest of his life and he was going to have to learn to control himself. But that it was just fine to look and admire.

"Thanks, Mama," he said, with his arms thrown around my neck. "I feel so much better. I was holding it in and holding it in and it hurt. I'm glad I talked to you because you had five brothers and you understand these things."

81

A few weeks later, I was dusting around in corners and crevices of his room and came across a page from one of my women's magazines. I shrieked. It was a full page ad for Viagra. See if I ever send him to after-school science class, I thought. Then I turned it over. It was a picture of a beautiful young woman in a bikini.

I'm not sure why I was so surprised since when he was just three, he asked me to buy him an Archie comic book. I was thrilled because I grew up reading Archie myself. Then I found him in the middle of the afternoon literally spent on his bed with the comic book resting on his belly, opened to a storyline and pictures of Veronica and Betty trying on bathing suits. The boy who would no more rest in the middle of the day and risk missing something than a frat boy at Spring Break was suddenly interested in taking "naps" on a regular basis.

"I need to dream about those girls, Mama," he explained as he climbed under the covers with his book.

You can't blame a boy for worshipping the female form so completely. I either have a Micheangelo on my hands or a Bill Clinton.

"The Weaker Sex"

It was in grade school, I believe, when I learned one of many valuable life lessons: "There will always be somebody bigger, smarter, faster, (you fill in the "er") than you." That and "Sticking a jawbreaker up your nose is not the best idea."

I watched Larry King Live the other night as he celebrated his 70th birthday with his two young sons, 4 and 3, sitting on his lap. I was so happy. Not because it was his birthday, but because there actually is a parent of small children older than I.

I was almost 44 when I gave birth to my first child, Cory and 46 when his little sister, came along. Another life lesson: "The second birth is so much easier than the first." I can completely attest to that. It's amazing how completely painless adoption can be. No morning sickness, no sciatica and the only thing swelling up was my heart when I laid my eyes on Shea Isabella Lane for the first time.

While I'm just getting used to the idea of being 50, I'm completely overwhelmed by the fact that my little baby girl will turn four in just a few days.

From the day we brought her home from the hospital, she was an absolute dream. It was almost as though she was telepathically telling us, "Please, no fuss. Just go about your business, feed me now and then and I'll be just fine." All those little poems about girls were written with Shea in mind—until she turned three.

It was like aliens came in the night and reprogrammed by darling angel. Her sweet, high-pitched, melodic tones turned into Linda Blair expletives. The only thing missing was the guacamole.

One morning I asked her to leave the bathroom so her brother could have some privacy. She stomped out of the room, slammed the door and snarled like a pirate, "I need my privacy toooooo!"

While she manages to give her parents a hard time, she shows a completely different face to the public. Men and women, boys and girls, small animals and selected insects find themselves completely taken by her. A killer smile and dreamy, brown eyes that bat at just the right increments melt even the most dispassionate hearts.

While the rest of her soccer team is battling the opponent at one end of the field, Shea is busy giggling and flirting with the referee at the other. With a dollar in her hand for popcorn, she returns from the snack bar with a large container full and the bill still tight in her fist.

"Mama, that boy said it was on the house," she beamed.

With mood swings that would make a sorority house seem balanced, she can go from cuddling and sweet in my arms to a furrowed brow and pouty lips that would make Mick Jagger jealous. She can be as frustrating as she is spellbinding.

At four in the morning she tiptoes in my room, completely naked and attempts to slip into my bed—-again. I'm tired and losing patience and ready to send her packing when she whispers, "Mama, I love you," and as though she has just said, "Open Sesame," the blanket opens up and I sweep her in. As we're drifting off to sleep, she whispers again, "We need a bigger bed."

She goes from torturing her older brother, to wrapping her arms around his neck and showering him with kisses as he pretends to protest. And, when it's necessary, she is his biggest defender.

"Don't yell at Cory, Mama," she told me, patting my hand, after I scolded him for some misdeed. "He's a good boy."

As I walk her to school each morning, I have learned to be patient as she literally stops and smells the flowers--and the bushes and rocks along the way, gently kissing them each. I have learned to accept this as part of who she is—although the time she kissed the stuffed bear at a la-de-da boutique after having eaten a lollipop, required me prying her lips off the toy and running from the establishment before we were discovered. Shea looked like the Wolfman, with patches of fur on her mouth and cheeks.

As we continue in our slow crawl to school, a jet screams overhead leaving behind a long and puffy white stream in its path, which delights her no end.

"Hi!" she calls out to the plane, waving her hand. "Thank you! Thank you for doing that for me."

I continue to be amazed at the joy she has brought into our lives. How someone so slight and so small, can have such a huge presence in the family. And how we have a complete stranger to thank for the most precious gift of our lives.

We take twice as long as we should to get to school, but I figure this is my investment in the future. Thirty years from now, when her tired, old mother shuffles along to the grocery store, or restaurant or casino, I predict my daughter will patiently walk at my side. That or kick me into the gutter. It all depends on her mood.

To my amazing daughter, Shea
On her 8th Birthday

When I heard
I simply cried
We got you!
Not from me as intended
But from One who seemed to know
How much
We needed you

I'd give you everything
Show you
Teach you
and so much more
But instead something
I never bargained for

You have taught Me
Brought me
Shown me
A new way
How extraordinary the ordinary
How joyous the day
How God is there
Peeking over the sunset

My heart aches with love
For you, my angel
The way it did for my mother

From one daughter to another
But oh-so vulnerable
More than I could have ever known

How do you do
What you do?
A r t i s t
Dancer
Animal Tamer
A Magical smile and
Chocolate eyes
That melt in my soul
A triple threat.

I thank that God for you every day
And look forward to countless birthdays
To love and cherish and learn from you
My amazing daughter, Shea.

JUDY LANE

Life in the Judy Lane

JUDY LANE

"Blackberry Blues"

Voodoo dolls, shrunken heads and other devices of the dark side, meet the Blackberry.

Paris Hilton isn't the only one who's had some rough times it seems. Let me explain that I'm not one of those baby boomers who are constantly reminiscing about the "good old days" when we didn't have seat belts or helmets and parents could share a Heineken with their kids every now and then--oh, wait, maybe that's just my family.

And, I'm more inclined to buy a Green Day DVD than order the Doo-Wop series from public television. But, even I must admit when instead of the promise of the future, new technology becomes the bane of my existence.

I never wanted this contraption in the first place, but I've been cajoled at work and home to "get with it!" And, so I reluctantly did. My cell phone was replaced with a thin, rectangular object the size of a cigarette case. Remember the good old days, when people used to carry cig...oh, sorry.

Anyway, the first thing I noticed is that the key pad was something out of Ripley's with each microscopic key serving multiple purposes, all to fit every conceivable symbol, letter, number and icon on the head of pin. I don't know about you, but my fingers are large enough to actually leave prints. Only a crow's claw could possibly peck these keys with any degree of efficiency.

This particular unit was given to me on a trial basis and so I haven't had all of my old information transferred yet. So, now I'm carrying the new job, the old cell with all the phone contacts and my personal phone because Pepper and I can call each other for "free." This, of course, is a euphemism for 99% of the calls she makes are to everyone except me, which explains the $200 monthly bill for all that "friends and family" stuff I've only heard rumor of.

The Blackberry can do it all—-email, download more ring tones than I have friends, take grainy, crime photos, give me the money exchange rate in eleven third-world countries and probably give a guy a prostate exam, but I can't seem to make a simple phone call. Mainly because I can't see the Lilliputian keyboard.

I punch in what I believe are the right numbers 555-027--and suddenly the 7 is repeated six times, 7777777. I try the delete key and then the entire readout turns into text: "Krxxnpapyuadsf!" It's probably Russian for "You ken't do it, ken you, nudnik!"

On my way to drop off the kids at camp, I put my nemesis in the cup holder and it automatically dialed Pepper. Forget that I have been trying unsuccessfully to dial her for about three days.

"I can't talk," she whispered. "I'm in a meeting."

"I'm not calling you. The phone is!" I screamed much to the delight of my children who are giggling at their mother's foibles.

Thankfully, she hung up because I had no idea how to do that and decided I would just let the battery die since theoretically that should disconnect me. I put the menace in its handy-dandy carrying case only to hear the phone redialing and a familiar voice,

"I said I can't talk! I'm in a meeting!"

I punch what I believe to be a hang-up key only to hear a recorded voice.

"Say a command."

Say what?

"Say a command," it demands.

I scream a certain popular obscenity and now the kids are hysterical with laughter.

"No command heard," it now reprimands me.

I've suddenly become an Adam Sandler movie to the kids who, as all those savvy techno giants would say, are ROTFLMAO.

I was given a Lamborghini when all I needed was a bicycle. And I believe with my initial reluctance and growing hostility, the Blackberry began to fight back. Much like the talking doll did to Telly Savalas on that Twilight Zone episode.

"I'm talking Tina and I'm going to kill you!"

I was rushing out the door late for a meeting, bags in hand. The Blackberry hanging on for dear life, earphones attached like an umbilical cord, the old phone with all the data and the "free" phone so I could call Pepper who was on the phone to everyone else in the country and, of course, the three sets of glasses I own, one for the computer, one for reading and the other to disguise myself so my boss won't recognize me when I'm leaving early. Bags and phones and glasses, oh my, and of course I need to use the restroom—now. Remember the good old days, when you could hold—

Anyway, I rush into the ladies room, drop all the equipment on the floor like a soldier back from battle, enter the duplex stall, do my thing and push the door back open only to have it fly off the hinges.

My natural instinct is to run and hope no one sees me. But, I must wash my hands--all those weird biohazards and such. So, now I'm even later, poised at the sink, bags, rags, and bottles waiting to be collected, the huge door hanging on by one single bolt and the possibility of a colleague walking in at any moment.

I quickly wash my hands and spin around to the techno-whiz "motion activated" towel dispenser. And nothing. I suspect the Blackberry has been talking to this thing.

I put my hands under the sensor. I wave my wet hands 'round and 'round like casting a spell. I do a Fonzie like it's a jukebox. I huff and I puff and nothing. Of course, the other day when I sneezed in the lobby, the thing started spitting out paper like a Pez dispenser on crack. But, not now. I wipe my hands on my pants like we used to in the old days, gather up my steamer trunk of gadgets and flee towards the exit only to drop my favorite pair of reading glasses on the ground and promptly crush them under foot.

I run screaming out of the bathroom and down the hall.

"The door's off its hinges!"

I would have called for help, but I would need a phone to do that. I could get the weather report in Zimbabwe or download stats on a potential new spouse from down under, but…well you know.

It's clear that if I were being attacked, instead of dialing 911, I would have to take the damn thing and hit the intruder upside the head with it. And, if I'm lucky, they would both fall into a million pieces on the ground.

As the Temps would say, "I ain't too proud to beg," or admit when I'm beat.

Remember the good old days, when we used to use two Dixie cups and a string…

"Woulda Shoulda Why I Oughta!"

What is it about some people who find the need to say whatever pops into their empty little heads? You know, like the one at work who directs his bony finger to the Jupiter-like bump in the middle of your forehead and makes an announcement on a bullhorn.

"You've got a pimple!"

Like he just discovered uranium. Did it really not occur to him that you obsessed in front of the mirror that morning, debating whether this would constitute a sick day?

You'd like to respond with something equally tactless, but, of course, you never do. Because like most of us, you were taught to be polite. "If you have nothing nice to say…" and all that sort of thing.

I had a co-worker study me carefully and then drone, "Your hair is flat."

"And so's your ass, but you don't see me issuing an email blast," I replied—in my fantasy. Because just like most decent people, I usually say something nice or nothing at all despite the fact that I have a tome of "shoulda saids," for occasions like this.

"Since you're a valued customer, we can lower your interest rate from 23.5% to 22%"

"Wow! That's very generous Don Guido."

"Gees! You're a <u>big</u> woman!"

"Excellent observation, my little Lilliputian. Now go climb a dandelion."

"Sorry, no public restrooms in this store."

"Okay, then I guess my daughter is going to have to pee on your shoe. Will that work?"

Instead, like most good people, I usually huff and puff as I rush off to find a place that will take a seven-year old with the bladder a size of a pea.

At what point do people decide to take on the role of narrators of life? And where do they get the list of comments they seem required to fulfill each day like a traffic cop's quota?

"You're fat," "You're skinny," "You've got a stain on your blouse/tie," "Your dog/kid/spouse needs a bath," "You've got a microscopic piece of lint on the bottom of your shoe."

I'm curious as to what effect they are seeking? When they run into an old friend at the mall and declare, "You've lost your hair!" do they expect him to clutch his scalp and run screaming through the center to see if he can find it?

My friend's mother when visiting insists on shouting "...phone's ringing!" despite modern technological advancements like that little bell cleverly installed in each unit. Perhaps Mom should get a job as a guide person for those with hearing disabilities. It's just a thought.

There are only a few instances in which such inane proclamations might be pertinent.

"<u>You're bleeding profusely</u>." It's possible you may not be aware that you've just been shot and need to seek medical attention right away.

For men: "<u>You're fly is open</u>." For women: "<u>Your skirt is tucked inside your pantyhose</u>." Oddly enough, even buffoons won't share this handy tidbit with another person, although it would be helpful to be spared the embarrassment/shame/legal complications that may arise.

"The train is coming." If you have stopped on the railroad tracks to ask a pedestrian for directions, it would be useful to know this.

"There's a rabid chipmunk sitting on your shoulder." Even those of us who are not campers would see the judiciousness of such a detail.

My goal is that when I turn a certain age—not sure which one that is, but I suspect it's fast approaching—I will actually blurt out all those shoulda-saids. I came quite close the other day.

I was in a clothing store when I saw an elderly gentleman assisting his equally elderly wife choose earrings. He was the cutest thing helping her match and knowing that she was a "clipper" and not pierced.

I noticed that he was wearing a Cal cap. I was wearing my UC San Diego t-shirt and suddenly we caught each other's eye.

"Are we rivals?" I asked playfully.

"I don't know," he smiled. "Are we?"

And then we proceeded to discuss the University system, his grandchildren and all the places he's lived since graduating college in 1958. Places he referred to as "settlements," which I found to be just precious. My enthusiasm with the man's charm was not lost on the Mrs. She looked at me with disdain. That, or she had severe gas, I'm not sure.

"Darling," he said cheerfully. "She's from San Diego!" Before I could extend my hand to greet her, she turned sharply at her beloved and snapped.

"Time to go!"

"Isn't that funny?" he continued. "We met another nice lady from San Diego at our hotel."

"Time to go!" she growled and took her darling by the arm as he waved over his shoulder.

"Nice meeting you both!" I called out. But, there was that "shoulda-said" just a percolatin' in my mind.

"Get real, sister. You think I'm gonna steal your husband? Aside from the fact that he probably dated Dolly Madison, I'm gay," and then plant a big wet-one on her lips.

But, good common sense, a sweet man who deserves so much more and the fact that he was much prettier than she, steered me toward the high road. But, it won't be long...

"On My Honor, I Will Do My Best To Be Prepared"

We've all seen them. The kits, the warnings, the broadcast advisories. Whether you're preparing for the storms of the East Coast or the earth swallowing you up in the West, you know the drill. Or at least you should by now.

You can buy your emergency kit for 500% markup or you can make your own. The gallons of water, the toiletries and canned food and, if you're like me, the essentials like wine and M&Ms.

But, where exactly do you keep this stuff? My car hasn't seen the inside of the garage since I moved in, so where on earth am I supposed to stack up the Apocalypse supplies? As it is, I have fourteen Easter egg coloring kits, all with missing pieces, three pumpkin carving kits and a dozen assorted Halloween, Christmas and Valentine's Day window appliqués that are all stuck together. Even if I had the supplies, I'd never be able to find them when I need them.

We just returned from four days away from home, including a trip to Universal Studios. Naturally, all I wanted to do was plop down in my easy chair and well, take it easy. No sooner had I cracked open my Pringles when there was a knock at the door and a notice that a water main had broken in a neighboring community and that our drinking water had tested positive for "E coli."

I heard loud organ music right out of Phantom when she said that. Okay, maybe it was just me.

There are certain two-word phrases that send chills down your spine: Taxes due. Relatives staying. Mel Gibson. But the mother of all has to be "E coli." Not to be confused with "Riiiiiiicola!" which is a good thing.

There was no need for panic—that's what the neighborhood watch lady said, anyway. But, I could see her eyes widening and spinning as she spoke. Or was it that after six years, she finally figured out who I was. Anyway, it was time to do something.

"Hurry! We need to get water. Everyone in the car!" I screamed.

Why I needed to load up the entire family like gypsies on the lamb, I don't know. But, the children obviously sensed something in my voice and my daughter Shea packed her bags and all her stuffed animals.

Normally, I wouldn't have been so tense about the whole thing. But, we just saw the back lot where "War of the Worlds" was filmed. The wreckage, the carnage—and that was just the public restroom. As if that wasn't enough, HBO was playing the movie in our hotel room. I saw what can happen when people get freaked. Tom Cruise packed heat because, "someone is going to want our car," he cautioned his children.

Would my gentile neighbors suddenly storm our car for the water? When I was seven, my sister and I were robbed of our moon pies by the neighborhood bully. So, who knows? Then, my older brother Mickie came to our rescue.

"Let's call Uncle Mickie!" I added. "Just in case."

We filled our cart with water of every configuration—the huge gallons containers, the kids' size and even some with flavoring. Then we drove home with the lights out so the vigilantes wouldn't see us.

The warnings were broadcast on our local stations. "Boil water." "Boil water." "Boil water." On every channel that was their best suggestion. I don't know about you, but I don't have 50-gallon cauldrons to boil any significant amount of water. I boiled the water in my teakettle that yielded four cups. I spill that much at dinner.

While the children were all nestled and snug in their beds, Mama was downstairs boiling water all night, looking for pitchers and bowls and anything to store the stuff. And suddenly, I was terribly thirsty. I couldn't get enough water.

"And don't look up the symptoms on the Internet!" Pepper shouted out to me.

Naturally, she was too late. When Neighborhood Watch lady said, "E..." I didn't wait for the "coli," before I pulled up my favorite—Mayo Clinic.

It's not that Pepper wasn't taking this seriously, it's just that she knows how impressionable I can be. When I was pregnant, she burned my copy of "What to Expect..." since I was convinced that I was giving birth to a two-headed alien beast. But, the final straw came when I was certain I had prostate cancer.

And, so we sit—on our cases of water—and wait for further notification. In the meantime, water's boiling, the kids are brushing with Cherry-flavored stuff and I'm, well, I'm beginning to feel a little queasy. Slight cramping. Rumblings down below. And so thirsty...

JUDY LANE

"You Oughta Be In Pictures"

Being a parent has given me a dramatically different perception of school than when I was the kid who was attending.

For example, I always thought "public" school meant that it was free. That my being taxed to death along with every other poor, working slob was allowing our kids to take advantage of a free K-12 education. That is until reality sets in.

A week doesn't go by without a flyer coming home with those three little words: "Checks payable to:" There's PTA dues, book fairs, "optional" newsletters, magazines, and class parties for every holiday known to man—(note: didn't "Arbor Day" go out when indoor plumbing came in?). I'm writing more checks than a CEO bribing Congressmen.

Remember those taxes to which I referred, apparently they're not quite enough to cover even the essentials. I'm not opposed to making up for some of these short-comings since my kids get an amazing education, but when I'm buying Windex, cases of toilet paper, and Kleenex to wipe other kids' chins, I'm beginning to get suspicious.

"What are you doing?" I asked Cory as he began ransacking the garage.

"The school is falling apart," he explained as he picked through the toolbox. "Do we have any nuts and bolts we can donate?"

Just when you've stocked the classroom, the kids come home with the class photos. Not just once, because apparently the school believes in the old saying, "three times the charm.

First, there's the "official" photo, which is just your kid sitting on a stool in front of a plain backdrop. For this you have to pay up front like you're pumping gas in a bad neighborhood at 2:00 a.m. "No money. No photo shoot."

You dress your darlings up in their best clothes, comb their hair just so and even spray it. You even have them practice that winning smile—the one you see all the time. The one that melts your heart and makes you agree to your daughter's request for chocolate cake for breakfast. The one that turns you into putty as you raise your son's allowance to something equivalent to state minimum wage. The one that everyone remarks about when they are introduced to your angels for the first time.

Then you get the photos back. Your children look as though they were inserted head-first into a turbo-engine wind tunnel. Instead of Shea and Cory and their winning smiles, you have Joan Rivers and Joe Pesci. Ah, wait; there is one with teeth showing. Now, you've got an 8x10 of Nanny McPhee.

You have to wonder about the photographer. Does he even speak to the children; much less say something remotely friendly that might cause them to actually give a half-way natural smile? I can just imagine this guy's profile on some on-line dating service with his "favorite things" including crime scene photos and aerial shots of landfills, with children and puppies under "things that stick in my craw."

You take a deep breath and pass these winners out only to those you have under the category of "will love my children no matter what," all the while explaining that those are "freckles—not warts!" And just when you think it's over for another year, you get yet another set of photos sent home.

These include your child's mug imbedded in everything from coffee cups and refrigerator magnets to tongue depressors and shoehorns. It's just a couple of dozen different ways to make you feel completely guilty about ever considering nixing these novelties. They're a tad better than the official photo because now your child is leaning up against a plastic tree of some kind to give a really natural look.

And finally, when you've covered the toaster, door jams and the car bumpers with stickers of your darlings, you get the mother of all pictures—the "Class Photo." This is one you must buy, according to your children, because it includes everyone in the class.

"She's my mortal enemy," Shea explains pointing to the face of a seemingly sweet child.

But instead of the ones we took when I was a kid that had you all lined up in rows, it's that "official" individual photo pasted into each of the 20 squares on the page.

You don't get to see the full perspective. The one kid who you accidentally mistake for the teacher since she's so much taller than the rest of the kids or the one whose eyes are rolling upwards as though he's spotted a ceiling lamp about to fall. Or the obviously mischievous little guy with a devilish smile who, from the looks of it, is probably pinching the kid next to him. Or the one they will print in the newspaper 20 years from now when one of these darlings grows up to be a serial killer.

"There. See it? He's got those beady eyes. The eyes of a killer."

Or any number of other real moments captured in that 10 seconds when they made you all line up together.

And so you write yet another check for an item that will end up at the bottom of a cardboard box somewhere in the garage. As you gaze across each child in each square you realize something very important. Your kid isn't the only one who looks like a stroke victim.

JUDY LANE

"Sugar and Spice and Everything Addictive"

It starts out quite innocently. You try your first one and think, "Well, it's just one. How much can it hurt?" Before you know it, you're having another and another. Soon, you're staying home, avoiding crowds just so you can have it. Hiding your stash from your spouse, the kids, anyone who may want in. Next, you're on the streets, disheveled and shaky with eyes glazed over, begging for it. It happened to me, my friend, and it can happen to you. So, when they ask you, just say no.

"No Girl Scout Cookies for me!"

Don't let those sweet little girls fool you. They're pigmy pushers in pigtails is all.

I was home one Saturday morning buffing my toenails when I heard at knock at my door. After three attempts to get up, I finally rolled myself to the door. I opened it to find two darling little angels smiling at me.

"Good morning!" said the little blondie. "Would you like to order some Girl Scout cookies?"

"Does the Pope wear little red shoes?" I replied as I sprung to my feet, which was no easy feat.

They stared blankly, but still smiling.

"Of course I do!" I screamed. "I'm addicted to the sugary treats, don't you understand?!"

I grabbed the order form from her tiny paws and checked off every one: Thin Mints, Samoas, Caramel deLites, Peanut Butter Patties, Tagalongs, Peanut Butter Sandwich, Do-si-dos, Shortbread, Trefoils. I didn't even know what half of these flavors were. But, believe me, if they offered Lizard Leg Drops, I'd take two.

"Now go!" I screamed as I sent the two little demons off to my unsuspecting neighbors.

I slumped back down in my easy chair and wiped the tears. "It's not your fault, Judy. They hooked you."

Just then, there was another knock at the door. I figured my neighbors heard the commotion and called the police. Instead, I found another cherubic-looking miniature mobster standing there with an order book.

"Would you like to—"

"Two of your henchmen were already here," I interrupted.

You'd think I just told her Hilary Duff stopped recording and moved to Somalia. A teardrop the size of Delaware began to form in the corner of one of her big, blue eyes. Just to avoid a scene, I was forced to order another set. As I watched the Bad Seed skip down my driveway, I noticed the other two were at the home of my elderly neighbor Mrs. McKnight. Just to put things into perspective, Mrs. McKnight's youngest son is on the National Board of Directors for AARP. It was clear that I had to protect this sweet little old lady from these pipsqueak peddlers.

"No!" I screamed as I approached McKnight's door. "Don't do it. They'll suck you in and then suck you dry. You'll spend your pension."

Apparently, Mrs. M has been stocking up on her Boost. When I came to, I was sprawled on her front lawn. I looked up to see her hugging the two tiny Jezebels.

When they're not infiltrating your neighborhood or commandeering the local grocery store, they're enlisting their parents to act as mules for the stuff. There isn't an office in America that doesn't have at least a dozen frazzled parents soliciting their co-workers. At one office where I used to work, a mother went so far as to post an 8x10 glossy of her child to further stir up the conscience. The fact that her daughter was 26 and serving 5-10 at Frontera for armed robbery was another story. We all bought the maximum.

The shipment is in. Today, family, friends, co-workers, the neighborhood syndicate, the strange little child imp who popped up under the stall in theatre restroom, they all came to collect. And, that's when it hits you. You've got two problems now. You've got to find a portable silo to stash your goodies and an equity loan to pay for your habit.

JUDY LANE

"The New Age"

"Fifty is the new 40!"
"Forty is the new 30!"
"Thirty is the new 20!"
At this rate, we'll all be rebirthing.

Are we really in better shape than our parents or do we just like to think we are? And how much does plastic surgery have to do with that youthful appearance we're coveting? I don't know about you, but I'd rather look my age than have my mug pumped with cow piss, stretched over the top of my head and shellacked like an antique end table.

Recently, I had a health appraisal. This was a two-appointment deal. I guess at my age, they've gotta take their time going over all the used parts.

Following the end of the first session, I received a three-page assessment of what they had discovered so far.

"Congratulations!" read the first line. "You are physically younger than your chronological age!"

"Ha!" I called to Pepper. "I'm younger than my real age!"

"What?" she exclaimed in disbelief. "There must be some mistake."

"You're just jealous because you're the real 43 not the new 43 or 33 or some'n or udder," I sputtered.

Then I read further into the assessment. I was praised for my excellent blood pressure and amazing lung capacity. The latter is something I recently discovered when I dipped into a pool and noticed that whether or not I moved my arms and legs, I managed to float quite well in the deep end. This is something that would have come in quite handy all those years I was worried about boat trips and cruises for fear of falling overboard and drowning. Who knew Molly Brown and I had so much in common. Mainly due to this unparalleled lung capacity I possess. But, I digress. Back to my assessment.

The cholesterol was okay and so were all the blood tests. My flaw, if you will, was my weight.

"Do you know what your BMI is?" the doctor asked.

I flushed as I assumed he was talking about personal bathroom habits that shouldn't be discussed in polite company or at least in the light of day.

"No, no," he chuckled, as if I were kidding. It's your body mass index."

Once he explained that little formula to me, I was ready not only to thump him on his pointy head with his little hammer thingy he uses for reflex tests, but to change the subject to just about anything else, including my bodily functions.

Without actually saying "Okay, listen here, Fat-Fatty. Lose weight or die!" he explained that my health would improve greatly if I were to handle this little problem.

Finally, the conclusion of my written appraisal:

"You are chronologically 53 years old, but good news, your current physical age is 52 years old! And, if I were to lose the weight of a small child or runway model, "...your age would be.... drum roll, please...51 years old!"

Well, whip out the Ben 'n Jerry's and crack up a brew. Whoop-de-friggin'-do. Am I really going to risk the seriously unpleasant humor which will envelope me and those who dare to cross my path when I am on a diet--for one lousy year off my rightful age?

Then it occurred to me that never having smoked, or been to rehab for drugs or other mind-altering substances of the liquid and pill variety, avoiding bacon and Streptococcal dogs (see: frankfurters) and overexposure to the sun has done practically nothing to improve the age factor. This was all very distressing not to mention making me extremely hungry.

While perusing my refrigerator for just the right thing to get me through this dip in the emotional roller coaster of my life, I had a revelation or two: 1) While it seems I can't drown, my sorrows definitely can with just the right mix of soft ice cream and crunchy toppings; 2) And since I'm 53, passing as 52, possibly on my way to 51, who knows what's possible?

So, as I spooned my way through a bowl of happy, I began to make a guest list for my next birthday. After all, big celebrations come with the big 5-0.

THE END

(Except for a few extra pictures…)

JUDY LANE

Judy at age 8 with sister Sally, big brother Mickie
and little brother Petie.

The Catholic Women: Judy's Mum, Aunt Nellie (the Nun)
and Auntie Margaret

Rabbinical students: Judy's father Harry and his brother Arnold

Cousin Father Peyton with his parents (kneeling)

L-R The Girls: Eleanor, Sally, Aunt Nelllie, Mum,
Auntie Margaret, and Judy

Judy & Pepper, 2008

Our Wedding Day: Judy, Cory, Pepper, & Shea
Legally Wed on September 8, 2008

Little Judy…Our Little Irish Jew…
who knew?

JUDY LANE

Made in the USA